Life Lessons for Littles

Janice Six

Photos by Julia Six Aldriedge

©2024 Janice Six

Photographs ©2024 Julia Six Aldriedge

Back cover (family photo), three generations: Ron Allen, son Jesse Allen, father Gene Allen

ISBN: 979-8-9873351-6-1

Published by Texas Star Trading Company
174 Cypress Street, Abilene, TX 79601
www.TexasStarTrading.com
(325) 672-9696

Design by Lauren Monsey, Monsey Creative LLC

Printed in the USA

This book is dedicated to

Greer Louise Six,

My namesake and first grandchild,

And to any additional grandchildren

We may be blessed to nurture in years to come.

Life Lessons for Littles

Table of Contents

A Great Resource for Families

As ministers, we are always on the lookout for good resources for families to use at home, whether prayers that can be said in the car or books that can be treasured for years to come. Even children who are in church every Sunday might only receive four hours of Christian education in a week, which is only about a tenth of the educational hours that they receive at school.

We both remember much of our earliest faith formation happening in the car. Whether it was praying on the way to day care or school in the morning or singing classic Sunday school songs on long drives, our journey from point A to point B also informed our journey of faith.

As we got older, we began to ask questions that our parents didn't always know how to answer. So, they gave us books full of questions that children typically ask like, "How did we get the Bible?" or "Why should I pray?" These books didn't answer all our questions, but they continued to guide us in our faith formation.

As much as we want children in church school and weekly programming, we are convinced that the most important element of a child's spiritual development happens at home. *Life Lessons for Littles* is a great tool to encourage at-home faith formation in an accessible and engaging way. We know that this book will touch the families in our own church and far beyond.

Carlo Sosa–Ortiz and Grace Sosa
Associate Pastors
First Central Presbyterian Church
Abilene, Texas

Introduction
Sharing Life Lessons with Children

When my children, Greg and Julia, were young, a friend of mine took delight in referring to them as "the Littles." It was her own unique term of endearment for them. Each time she asked, "How are the Littles?" it made me smile. Over time, I found myself referring to other children in this charming way.

So, when encouraged to compile a collection of life lessons that could be shared with children, this sweet memory came to mind. Thus, I have chosen to entitle this collection *Life Lessons for Littles*.

Yes, I know that some children might balk at being referred to as "little" since even by age 4 they prefer to think of themselves as "big," so hopefully one of the first rhymes, "Let the Littles Come to Me," will help them understand that being a "Little" is a wonderful blessing!

The rhymes, questions and prayers are written to be shared orally with children ages 4 to 10 years by parents, grandparents, teachers, and other caring adults. It is my hope that *Life Lessons for Littles* will provide an opportunity for meaningful conversations and teachable moments between those whose influence is great in young lives and the Littles in their care.

Janice Six

Pass the Faith, Please

*(For parents, grandparents, teachers,
and others with Littles in their care)*

Ah, that faith were mashed potatoes,

Cream-style corn or ripe tomatoes,

Offered from a table of oak,

Common food for common folk.

Ah, that faith grew on a vine,

Grapes and berries ripened with time.

A sprinkle of sugar,

Splash of cream,

Nature's best needs not a thing.

Ah, that faith were ours to serve,

Double portions heaping high,

Seconds…thirds…want some more?

Plenty stocked behind the pantry door.

Lest a child refuse to dine,

Faith could be force-fed with time.

Bless the child who craves the taste,

Bowl scrapped clean with none to waste,

No sweeter words are there than these:

"Pass the faith, please."

Sparks

• What can you do to whet the appetite of Littles entrusted to your care to give them a hunger for learning about God?

• What do you hope your Littles learn from you about God?

Prayer

Gracious God,
You have entrusted these precious Littles to our care,
With intentionality may we faithfully share
What we know of you through all we say and do.
Freely and generously may we extend your love,
Exuding gratitude and joy in all our actions,
Exercising patience and kindness
With every reaction.
Help us be slow to anger and quick to forgive,
And when we fall short,
May we promptly be willing to apologize.
Teach us and guide us in your ways,
As we seek to lead these Littles,
Praying they never stray.
Amen.

Hear, O Israel: The Lord is our God, the Lord alone. You shall love the Lord your God with all your heart, and with all your soul, and with all your might. Keep these words that I am commanding you today in your heart. Recite them to your children and talk about them when you are at home. And when you are away, when you lie down and when you rise. Bind them as a sign on your hand, fix them as an emblem on your forehead, and write them on the doorposts of your house and on your gates.

Deuteronomy 6:4–9

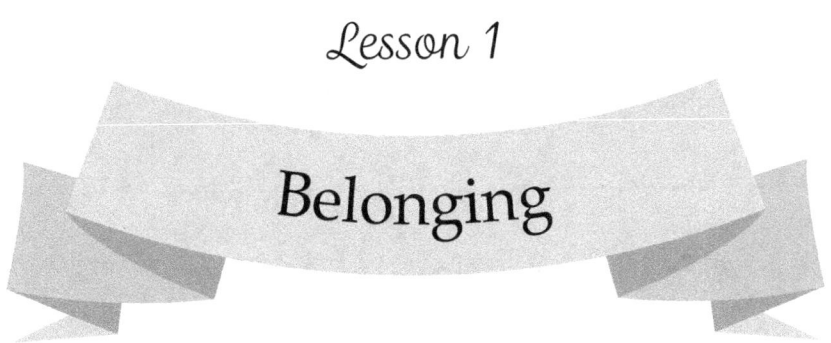

Belonging

Let the Littles Come to Me!

People were bringing little children to him in order that he might touch them; and the disciples spoke sternly to them. But when Jesus saw this, he was indignant and said to them, "Let the little children come to me; do not stop them; for it is to such as these that the kingdom of God belongs. Truly I tell you, whoever does not receive the kingdom of God as a little child will never enter it." And he took them in his arms, laid his hands on them, and blessed them.

Mark 10:13–16

We All Belong

See what love the Father has lavished on us that we should be called children of God; and that is what we are.

I John 3:1–3

Let the Littles Come to Me!

"Jesus is here! Jesus is here!"

All the people chant and cheer.

Mothers walk quickly, their babies in arms.

Dads dash briskly, toddlers perched on their shoulders.

Everyone is eager to greet the miracle man Jesus.

But who does Jesus want most to see?

The Littles — young ones--not yet able to climb a tree!

Jesus shouts to his friends controlling the crowd,

"Let the Littles come to me!

The kingdom of God belongs to these."

Pharisees and grown-ups scratch their heads,

"The kingdom of God belongs to these?"

Jesus replies, "Become like Littles, with a faith so pure,

and the kingdom of God will also be yours."

Many lessons we can learn from the Littles,

But a child-like faith is the most treasured of all.

Sparks

- Why did Jesus get upset with the disciples?

- What did Jesus do to show that little children are important to God?

- What does it mean to have faith?

Prayer

Thank you, Jesus, for noticing little children and inviting them to come and sit with you. Thank you for letting everyone know that little children are special to God. Amen.

We All Belong

Food and water,

Sleep and shelter,

All are a must for healthy bodies,

But what we need doesn't end with these.

Knowing we are never alone,

Knowing we are forever loved,

And knowing that we truly matter,

This is what satisfies the soul.

The key to a happy life is knowing,

Who we are and to whom we belong.

We all need to belong,

We all need people to call our own,

We all need a place to feel at home.

I know the place where you belong,

I know the people to call your own.

I know the One who loves you forever,

I know the One to whom you belong.

Come with me,

And I'll take you home.

Sparks

• Who are the people who belong to you?

• Where are a few places you feel comfortable, accepted, and at home?

• Where do we all belong, and to whom do we all belong?

Prayer

Heavenly Father, thank you for claiming us as your children and loving us forever. Thank you for making us part of the church family, where we can experience your love by caring for each other. Amen.

Lesson 2

Compassion

Compassion Tugs at the Heart

Rejoice with those who rejoice, weep with those who weep. Live in harmony with one another; do not be haughty, but associate with the lowly; do not claim to be wiser than you are.

Romans 12:15–16

Let's Get Dressed

As God's chosen ones, holy and beloved, clothe yourselves with compassion, kindness, humility, meekness, and patience. Bear with one another and if anyone has a complaint against another, forgive each other… Above all, clothe yourselves with love, which binds everything together in perfect harmony.

Colossians 3:12–14

Compassion Tugs at the Heart

What does it mean to have compassion?

Is it a fruit, a rash, or a fashion?

No, my friend, it's none of these,

Yet it's sweet like a peach, painful at times,

And as warm as a sweater in chilly weather.

Compassion's a feeling that tugs at the heart,

When someone is scared or falling apart,

It prompts us to action,

To help how we can,

Or simply stand still and hold their hand.

Compassion is patient and often wise,

Listening to others with tears in our eyes.

Imagining their pain and how they might feel,

When times are uncertain and burdens are real.

Compassion is kindness we carry inside,

It tugs at the heart and there it abides.

Sparks

- Do you remember a time when you felt sad for someone when something bad happened to him or her? What happened and what did you do or say?

- When have you given a hug or helped someone who was hurt or crying?

- What does it mean to you when we say, "Compassion tugs at the heart?"

- Who is sad or in pain that we can pray for right now?

Prayer

Thank you, God, for filling our hearts with compassion. Thank you for nudging us to care when others are hurting or sad. Please help _____ know we care. Help us to know how best to help. Amen.

Let's Get Dressed!

We are God's children,

One and all,

Loved inside and out,

Without a doubt!

What a precious gift it is,

To know that we are God's kids!

The best way to love God,

Is to love one another.

Like deciding what clothes to wear,

We get to choose our attitude.

So… Let's get dressed!

Clothe yourself with true compassion,

Choosing to care is always in fashion,

Through your eyes let kindness shine,

Keeping other's needs in mind.

Some problems are heavy and hard to bear,

All you need do is simply be there.

Wearing our feelings on our sleeves,

Means easily getting out of sorts,

Our feelings get hurt,

And we push friends away.

This is not how God would have us play.

Just as the Lord has forgiven us,

We, too, are asked to forgive each other.

Apologize and really mean it,

Ask for forgiveness,

And always be willing to give it.

Over all of these, choose to wear love,

Like a flowing cape or a warm cozy coat,

Love draws us together and fills us with hope.

Sparks

• If you had a coat made of love, what would it look like?

• How is putting on your attitude like putting on clothes?

• What is one of the best ways to love God?

Blessing

May the peace of Christ rule in your heart;

The word of Christ enrich your life;

May you treasure wisdom and humbly share it;

And with great thanksgiving,

Sing! Sing! Sing!

Sing to God with grateful hearts.

Whatever you do,

Whatever you say,

Bring glory to God in every way!

Lesson 3
Contentment

Making the Most of What We Have

Keep your lives free from the love of money and be content with what you have; for he has said, "I will never leave you or forsake you." So, we can say with confidence, "The Lord is my helper; I will not be afraid. What can anyone do to me?"

Hebrews 13:5–6

The Present

This is the day that the Lord has made; let us rejoice and be glad in it!

Psalm 118:24

...Give your entire attention to what God is doing right now, and don't get worked up about what may or may not happen tomorrow. God will help you deal with whatever hard things come up when the time comes.

Matthew 6:34 (The Message)

Making the Most of What We Have

Being happy with what we have,

Is what it means to be content,

Whether sleeping in a motor home,

Or camping in a tent.

When we're happy with what we have,

We feel at peace wherever we sleep.

Being content means being satisfied

With shoes that easily slip on our feet,

Or sneakers with laces that must be tied.

Being happy with what we have

Is enjoying our favorite ice cream

From a cup or a cone,

Without a wistful sigh

Or grumpy groan.

Being content

When everything goes our way

Is easy on any day,

But learning to be content

When things don't go as we intend,

Is learning to make the most of what we have,

Whether we're happy or sad.

Sparks

- What does it mean to be content?

- When things don't go the way you want, what do you say to yourself to be able to accept things the way they are?

- What does it mean to "make the most" of what we have?

Prayer

Dear God, thank you for all the gifts you have given us. Remind us to be grateful for what we have. On days when we don't get our way, help us to make the most of what we have and be content anyway. Amen.

The Present

Sun's up, let's play!

"This is the day the Lord has made,

Let us rejoice and be glad in it!"

This very moment is a gift from above,

We call it the present,

Because it's given with love.

With each second that passes,

We're given the choice:

Unwrap the present,

Reveal the splashes of joy,

It has to offer,

Or waste the moment,

Looking over our shoulders,

Regretting what's already done,

Or looking ahead,

Worrying about what's yet to come.

Accept the present as it is,

Open the gift,

And really live!

Sparks

• How do you feel when someone gives you a wrapped gift?

• How do you think you'd feel if you gave someone a gift and the person ignored it—didn't choose to open it?

• What is something we can celebrate in this very moment?

Prayer

God, you are the giver of all good gifts. Remind us, that the present—this very moment—is a gift from you. With joy, may we accept it and live every split-second of it! Amen.

Courage

Don't Be Afraid

Do not be afraid, little flock, for it is your Father's good pleasure to give you the kingdom.

Luke 12:32

Pray for Courage

I hereby command you: Be strong and courageous; do not be frightened or dismayed, for the Lord your God is with you wherever you go.

Joshua 1:9

Don't Be Afraid

It's easy to say but hard to do:

"Don't be afraid."

God said it often to prophets of old,

Angels spoke these words to shepherds we're told.

Certainly, Mary and Joseph were encouraged

When they heard,

"Do not be afraid."

Jesus assured the disciples caught in a storm,

And later as they huddled behind locked doors,

"Take heart. It is I. Do not be afraid."

Even Saul, who eventually became Paul, was told by God,

"Do not be afraid. I am with you,"

For there was work God wanted him to do.

So, even grown-ups can be afraid.

No matter our age or the reason we're scared,

God wants us to know God cares.

Sparks

• Have you ever been afraid? What did you say? What did you do?

• How could you help a friend who's afraid?

Prayer

Help me, God, I'm afraid. Amen.

Pray for Courage

New can be scary,

This is true.

New schools with new rules,

New teachers and new routines,

New friends with new names to learn,

New everything!

Learning something new can be scary, too.

Learning to play the piano,

Swing a bat,

Kick a soccer ball,

Or learning to tap.

Until we practice time and again,

It still makes us nervous each time we begin.

It takes lots of courage

To tackle what's new.

Without someone to give us a nudge,

It's highly unlikely we'll be willing to budge.

So, first ask God for a new attitude,

Then pray for courage to make the first move.

Sparks

- When have you been scared to try something new?
- Who helped you have the courage to try something new?
- If you've ever been to a new school, what was scary about it and what did you do?

Prayer

Loving God, just knowing you are always with us, even though we can't see you, gives us the courage to do what we must to tackle something new. Thank you for helping us face the future unafraid. Amen.

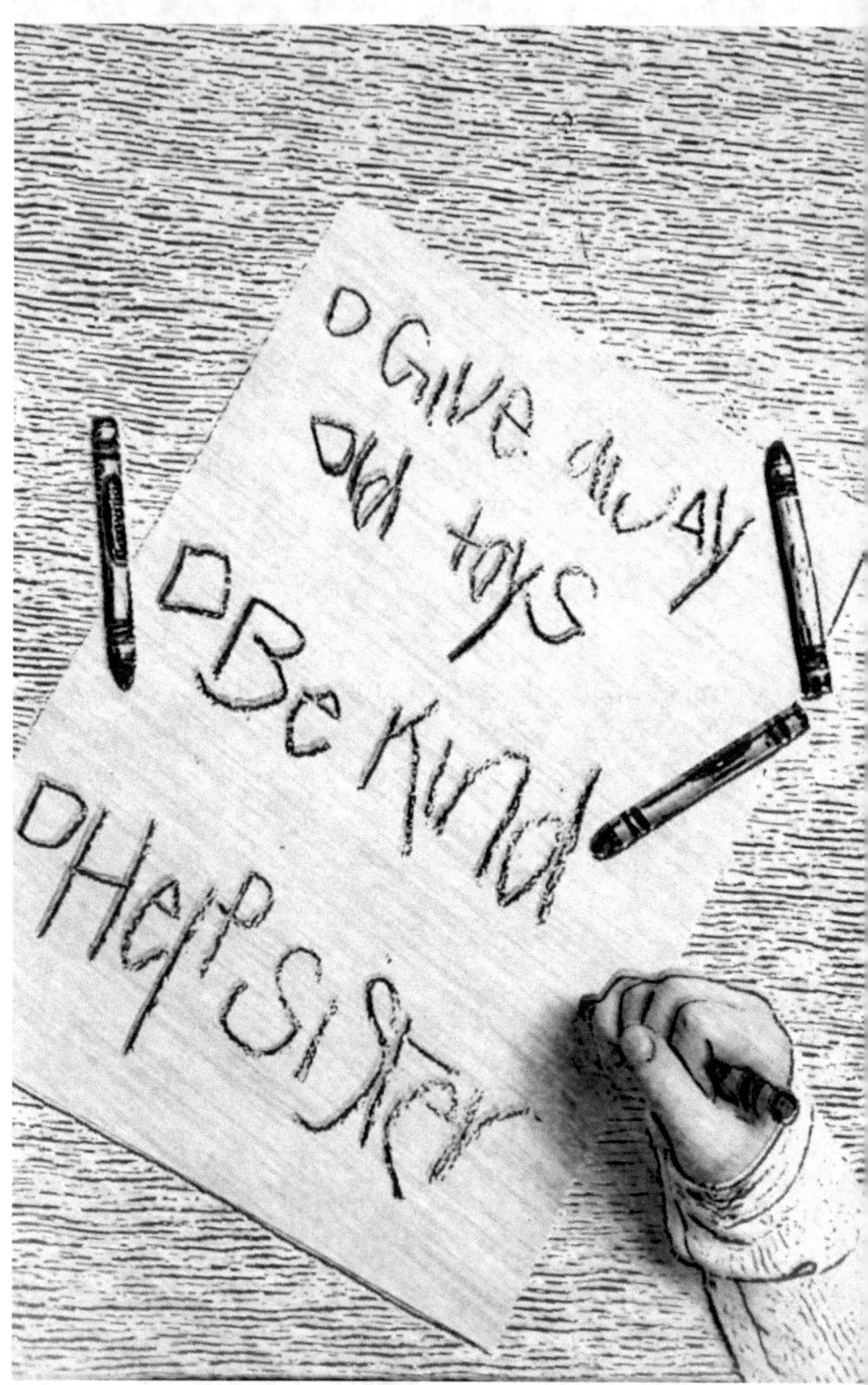

Faithfulness

Faith in Action

Dear friends, do you think you'll get anywhere in this life if you learn all the right words but never do anything? Does merely talking about faith indicate that a person really has it?... Faith and works, works and faith, fit together hand in glove.

James 2:14-17 (The Message)

Faith in Action

Good intentions are what we plan to do,

But good intentions only go so far,

They can make it to the list,

And maybe earn a star,

But until we get around to doing them,

They're nothing more than empty words.

We can boast all day of what we plan to do,

Like give away clothes we never wear,

Share toys with someone,

Who has none to spare.

But until we put our plan into action,

It's nothing more than empty words,

We've said before.

Lists can be helpful reminders

Of what to do, where to go, who to see,

And what we need.

But unless we do what's on the list,

We miss the point and waste the paper.

God expects more than plans and intentions,

God wants us to move into action!

Next time you feel inspired to help a friend,

Lend a hand, or do a good deed,

Just do it without wasting time,

Do it while it's still on your mind.

Do it before you push it aside,

Just go ahead and get around to it!

Sparks

- What is an intention?

- What is something you can do today to help someone?

- What is preventing you from doing it?

Prayer

Dear God, please forgive us when our good intentions and plans are nothing more than empty words. Prompt us to put our plans into action and do our part to share your love with others and make this world a better place. Amen.

Forgiveness

Words Hurt

To watch over mouth and tongue is to keep out of trouble.

Proverbs 21:23

Grudges

Put away from you all bitterness and wrath and anger and wrangling and slander, together with all malice, and be kind to one another, tenderhearted, forgiving one another, as God in Christ has forgiven you.

Ephesians 4: 31–32

Words Hurt

Sticks and stones may certainly break bones,

But words shoot darts straight to the heart.

Words do damage every day,

When we choose to use them in hurtful ways.

Words written or spoken are not easily erased,

From the eyes that see them,

And the ears that hear them,

They always leave a trace.

Saying "I'm sorry" only goes so far,

Sadly, these words seldom make it to the heart.

Even if we could take back what was said,

Scars remain, just the same.

Offering an apology is what we must do,

But there's no guarantee it will be received.

A much greater chance of being heard

Is remembering:

"Actions speak louder than words."

If something can be done to fix the damage,

Waste no time in taking advantage

Of any opportunity

To admit your mistake

And do what you can to set things straight.

Sparks

- When has someone said something that hurt you?
- What helped you feel better?
- When have you hurt someone with your words?
- What did you do to apologize?
- What does it mean to forgive someone?

Prayer

Words are powerful, God, and we can easily use them to hurt each other. Please forgive us when we speak words that are cruel or untrue. Give us the courage to apologize and ask for forgiveness. Amen.

Grudges

Lugging around a grudge is back breaking work,

Grudges are clunky and gnarly,

Heavy and cantankerous.

Grudges are nosey and noisy,

Stirring up trouble every chance they get.

Grudges poke and prod us to take revenge,

Pick a fight and never give in.

Stubbornly hold on with all our might,

The tighter we hold the heavier they grow.

Grudges feed on spoiled memories,

And other's mistakes,

Gnawing on words that make tempers flare,

Daring us to say and do,

What we know is neither good nor fair.

Grudges can live for years and years,

Making us miserable and robbing us of love,

Unless we are strong enough,

To do what we must.

It takes lots of strength to pry a grudge loose,

It might mean a willingness to call a truce,

Another way is choosing to say

These three difficult words:

"I forgive you,"

Then trusting in God to help this come true.

Sparks

- What is a grudge?
- How do grudges get on our backs?
- What is the danger of allowing a grudge to stay on our back?
- What can we do to get a grudge off our back?

Prayer

Dear God, sometimes my feelings get hurt and I get mad at someone. Help me to have the courage to talk to the person and set things right before a grudge crawls onto my back. Give me the strength to knock a grudge off before it makes my life miserable. Help me to forgive others' mistakes or the wrong they have willingly done. Amen.

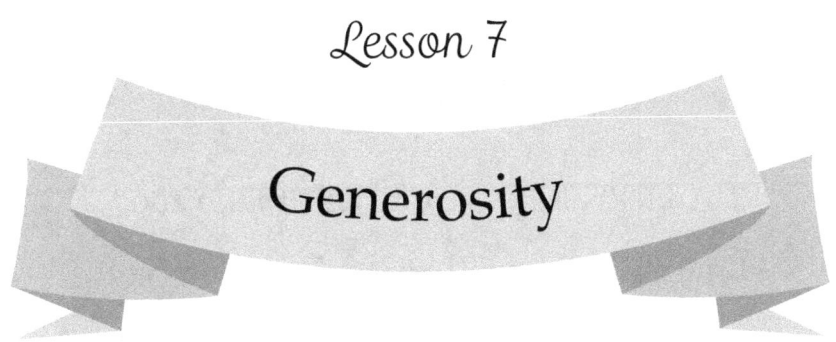

Generosity

Gift Giving

In all this I have given you an example that by such work we must support the weak, remembering the words of the Lord Jesus, for he himself said, "It is more blessed to give than to receive."

Acts 20:35

Sharing Is Caring

Those who are generous are blessed, for they share their bread with the poor.

Proverbs 22:9

Gift Giving

A kickball, toys, or tickets to the zoo,

I'm thrilled when I get to share with you.

Even a smile, a joke, or a "How do you do?"

All are gifts from me to you.

It's funny to think and hard to explain,

But the more I give,

The more I gain.

There's a happy feeling deep inside,

Each time I share,

I feel it rise,

It's like my body is about to explode,

Overflowing with confetti from head to toe!

Bubbling up, it bursts out as laughter,

Filling the room from floor to rafters.

All who are present are touched by the joy,

It's a beautiful sight and sound to behold.

No doubt, it's true, what I've been told:

More blessed are we to give than to receive.

Finally, what I have found:

Giving brings out the best in me,

Sharing with others is ecstasy!

Sparks

- What do you like to share with friends?
- How does it make you feel inside when you share?
- What is something a friend has given you that brought you joy?

Prayer

God, you are the giver of all good gifts. Thank you for the gifts you've given us, like laughter, joy, and kindness. Teach us how to freely share these gifts with others. Amen.

Sharing Is Caring

Sharing is a way to make friends,

Whether you're ten or ninety-two,

Sharing is a kind thing to do.

Almost anything can be shared,

It's a simple way to show you care.

Sharing a word of encouragement,

Or sharing a piece of cake over lunch,

Sharing scissors when making a craft,

Or telling a joke and sharing a laugh,

All are ways to share what you have.

Sharing with friends and family,

Is easy to do,

But what God expects of me and you

Is sharing with any who have a need,

Even those we might not know.

Everyone needs food and water,

Everyone needs shelter in a storm,

When cold winds begin to blow,

Everyone needs a warm place to go.

Everyone needs clothes to wear,

And those who are sick need medical care.

Not any of us can meet

All the needs of everyone,

But when we're willing

To work together,

Each sharing a little of this,

Or a little of that,

We can make a big difference,

And that's a fact.

Sparks

• What is something you enjoy sharing with a friend?

• What is something you can share with someone who is hungry?

• What is something you can share with someone who is cold?

• What is something your church family shares to help people in need?

Prayer

Dear God, thank you for the many blessings you have given us. Thank you for giving us opportunities to share with people in need. Thank you for giving us generous hearts and helping hands. Amen.

Gratitude

Two Simple Words

And let the peace of Christ rule in your hearts, to which indeed you were called in the one body. And be thankful.

Colossians 3:15

Thank You for Saying Thank You

Rejoice always, pray without ceasing, give thanks in all circumstances; for this is the will of God in Christ Jesus for you.

I Thessalonians 5:16–18

Two Simple Words

Gratitude begins with two simple words,

Words we're taught at an early age,

Simple words we're expected to say.

Long before our hearts feel grateful,

We've learned words that mean we're thankful.

When paid a compliment,

We mimic our parents,

Without wasting time,

Responding as they'd have us do,

With two simple words:

"Thank you!"

Thank you for this,

And thank you for that,

We've learned to say,

"Thank you"

At the drop of a hat!

Each "thank you" we say,

Makes us better in this way:

It alters our attitude,

Like drops of water,

On seeds of gratitude,

Planted deep within our hearts,

Gratitude slowly gets its starts.

Then one fine day,

We simply say,

"Thank you,"

And from the tone of our voice,

We suddenly know,

The seeds--first sown long ago--

Have burst into bloom.

Their fragrance fills every room of our hearts!

Suddenly, the two simple words

We were taught from the start,

Are feelings we cherish,

Deep in our hearts.

Sparks

• What are the two simple words we say when we're grateful?

• What are a few things for which you're grateful?

Prayer

Thank you, God, for our family and friends. Thank you for helpers, like _____ and _____. Thank you for making the world a beautiful place. Amen.

Thank You for Saying Thank You!

Each time I hear you say, "Thank you"

My heart swells with pride!

You see, I know what's growing,

Deep inside.

I hear you say "thank you"

All over town,

No doubt, your gratitude is growing,

By leaps and bounds!

Thank you for saying "Thank you"

To all of these folks:

Thank you to all who laugh at your jokes,

Thank you to friends for taking turns,

Thank you to teachers for helping you learn,

Thank you to grandparents for holding your hand.

Thank you to the director of the community band.

Thank you to the veterinarian for caring for your pets.

Thank you to the janitor for warning when floors are wet.

Thank you to the zookeeper for feeding the birds.

Thank you to the preacher for sharing God's word.

On and on the list goes,

The older you get the longer it grows.

Someday when you're on your own,

And I'm no longer around,

May you still be saying,

"Thank you" all over town.

When you do, I pray you'll hear,

An echo of my jubilant cheer:

"Thank you for saying thank you!"

And may these few words forever be,

Music to your ears.

Sparks

• Who are the first people to whom you'd like to say "thank you" right now?

• How can we say "thank you" to people who are not present?

Prayer

Thank you, God, for creating us to be thankful.
Remind us to say "Thank you" every day. Amen.

Lesson 9

Helpfulness

Helping Hands and Caring Hearts

Whatever you do in word or deed, do everything in the name of the Lord Jesus, giving thanks to God the Father through him.

Colossians 3:17

The Brownie Story

Therefore, my beloved, be steadfast, immovable, always excelling in the work of the Lord, because you know that in the Lord your labor is not in vain.

I Corinthians 15:58

Helping Hands and Caring Hearts

Helping hands and caring hearts,

They go together like a hand and glove,

Both are motivated by love.

Hearts feel the passion and pain of another,

Hands discover what they can do

To fashion a solution or two.

Helping hands can bake a cake,

Give a hug or a warm handshake.

Hearts that care are eager to share,

Whether it be a word of cheer,

Or letting a friend share a fear.

Helping hands apart from caring hearts,

Can do the job but lack the joy.

Caring hearts without helping hands,

May find it hard to give expression,

to what they feel.

Together, helping hands and caring hearts

Are a pleasing combination,

And a great place to start.

Sparks

• What is something your hands can do to help a friend?

• When has your heart inspired your hands to do something good for someone else?

• What is an example of Jesus using his helpful hands and caring heart to help someone?

Prayer

Thank you, God, for giving us hearts to love and hands to help. May the love in our hearts overflow into our hands so that all we do may become expressions of your love. Amen.

The Brownie Story

By the time she was four,

Julia could whip up a batch of brownies,

Without a drop of batter hitting the floor.

Standing on a chair to reach the counter,

She whisked and stirred with all her might.

Often the batter would slosh from the bowl,

But not even that seemed to matter.

Making brownies with her mom was pure delight!

There were times when Mom was in a hurry,

Times she was tempted to take the spoon

From Julia's tiny hand,

But then she'd see the pride in Julia's eyes,

As she whisked and stirred with all her might,

And Mom would stop herself and step aside.

One day while making a batch of brownies,

Julia's mother had a revelation:

God doesn't need us to do the work,

Nothing is impossible for God.

In the blink of an eye, God could make

The whole world a perfect place!

But God sees the joy it brings us

To help carry out God's plan,

So, like Mom, God steps aside and

Welcomes our helping hands!

Patiently, our Heavenly Father watches and waits,

As we fumble to do what we do,

And make what we make.

It's a joy to work alongside our Heavenly Father.

It's a joy to serve in Christ's name.

It's a joy to bake brownies with Mother,

And a joy to make the world a better place!

Sparks

• What is something one of your parents, grandparents or older brother or sister has taught you to do?

• How does it make you feel when you get to work alongside them?

• What is something you do with God's help?

Prayer

Dear God, You have given us helping hands, grateful hearts, and joy as we serve in Christ's name. Thank you for loving us enough to let us help you make this world a better place. Amen.

Lesson 10

Honesty

Honesty Wins

One who gives an honest answer gives a kiss on the lips.

Proverbs 24:26

"Just Kidding!"

…For learning about wisdom and instruction…let the wise also hear and gain in learning, and the discerning acquire skill, to understand a proverb and a figure, the words of the wise and their riddles.

Proverbs 1:1–6

Breaking Rules, Man Oh Man!

You shall not steal.

Exodus 20:15

Honesty Wins

Being honest means telling the truth.

Whatever you do,

Whatever you know,

Telling the truth is the way to go.

Honesty isn't always simple.

Admitting a mistake

You didn't intend to make,

Or confessing a wrong

You knowingly did,

It may be tempting to tell a fib.

Call it little or admit it's big,

One way or another,

The truth is this:

Most lies get back to your mother.

Now you're in trouble, that's for sure!

Discipline can be a super rough cure,

But here's the truth that's really tough:

You've damaged the trust of the ones you love,

You've tarnished your name,

And there's no one to blame.

So, remember this:

It takes time to earn what's lost,

Telling lies comes at a very high cost.

In the end honesty wins.

Sparks

• What is a reason someone might be tempted to lie?

• How does it make you feel when you hide the truth from your family?

• Who do you trust to tell if you've told a lie and now want to tell the truth?

Prayer

We know that telling the truth is what you want us to do, God. Please forgive us when we're not honest with people we can trust. Give us the courage to admit when we've done something wrong. Amen.

"Just Kidding!"

"Just kidding!" can be a tricky thing to say,

If you stretch the truth

To simply get your way,

This really isn't kidding and

It may be seen as fibbing.

"Just kidding!" only works

When it's said to make a joke

And no one gets hurt.

The key is saying, "Just kidding!"

Before anyone has time

To think you mean it,

Or else you'll be accused of lying,

And no one – especially you --

Will be amused.

"Just kidding!" can be a fun way to play,

If you follow these rules

Anytime you say it.

Sparks

- What do you need to remember when saying, "Just kidding!" so you won't be accused of fibbing?

- When is it inappropriate, or wrong, to say, "Just kidding!"?

- If I were to say, "There's a Zombie sneaking up behind you!" is this a good time to say, "Just kidding!" or not? Why or why not?

- If I were to say, "Your freckles look like pinto beans!" is this a good "Just kidding!" joke or not? Why or why not?

- Let's practice. You ask me a "Just kidding!" joke.

Prayer

Dear God, we just want to have fun. Help us to know the difference between saying something funny and saying something that might cause others to think we're fibbing. Help us think before we speak so we don't say something that might hurt someone's feelings. Amen.

Breaking the Rules, Man Oh Man!

"Ooh, la-la," whispers a little voice in your head.

See something you want?

"TAKE IT!"

That's what the tempter says.

"Touch it…"

"Hold it…"

"Imagine it's yours…"

Before you know it,

You've broken the rules!

In the blink of an eye, you've taken

Something that isn't yours.

Candy from the counter,

A toy from someone's hand,

Money from your mother's purse,

Man, oh man!

It happens so fast,

It's easy to do,

But there's a high price to pay for breaking the rules.

The candy, the toy, the money you steal,

Are never worth how guilty you feel.

Next time you're tempted to break the rules,

Repeat this little prayer and don't be fooled:

"Help me, Jesus, do no wrong.

I am weak, but you are strong. Amen"

Sparks

- What broken rule is this poem about?

- Why is it wrong?

- What is the "high price" we pay when we break this rule?

- What can we do when we are tempted to do wrong?

Prayer

Loving God, help us to know right from wrong. Give us the courage to choose what is right and pleasing in your sight. When we are tempted, give us the strength to walk away. Amen.

Hopefulness

Hoping and Wishing

But if we hope for what we do not see, we wait for it with patience.

Romans 8:25

Hoping and Wishing

Wishing and hoping,

Hoping and wishing,

The two are not the same.

Wishing is what we do

When we gaze upon a star.

Hoping is what we say

When we bow our heads to pray.

Wishing relies on happenchance,

Hoping trust in God above

To hear our prayers and act with love.

Hoping calls on us to do our part,

This often means we first must start

To listen, watch, and wait,

Before stepping out on faith.

Hoping is believing

The best is yet to come.

Sparks

- What is something you hope will happen soon?

- What is something you can do to help what you hope comes true?

Prayer

Dear God, you know all our hopes and dreams. Please let us know how we can help them come true. Thank you for guiding us as we step out in faith to do our part. Amen.

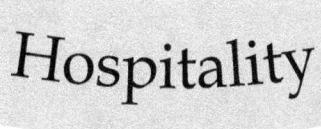

Hospitality

Friendship Circle

Some friends play at friendship, but a true friend sticks closer than one's nearest kin.

Proverb 18:24

Company's Coming

Whoever welcomes you welcomes me, and whoever welcomes me welcomes the one who sent me…and whoever gives even a cup of cold water to one of these little ones in the name of a disciple—truly I tell you, none of these will lose their reward.

Matthew 10:40, 42

Room at the Table

It is I, Jesus, who sent my angel to you with this testimony for the churches… The Spirit and the bride say, "Come," and let everyone who hears say, "Come." And let everyone who is thirsty come. Let anyone who wishes take the water of life as a gift.

Revelation 22:16–17

Friendship Circle

A friendship circle may begin with two,

And then it swells beyond a few.

One friend invites someone new,

Then a second friend

Wants to come along, too.

Now the circle is up to four.

Before we know it,

The friendship circle is bursting

Out the door!

The miracle of a friendship circle

Is how it expands like a rubber band.

Stretching our arms out open wide,

Reaching to touch the fingers of another,

We welcome all to join the circle.

The circle has no beginning or end,

There's always room to add a friend.

Just take a step back to create the space,

Put a smile upon your face,

And with a warm word of welcome

Invite the friend to take their place.

The beauty of a friendship circle

Is looking every person in the eye,

Standing in a great big circle,

Everyone is equal.

Sparks

- Who are people in your friendship circle?

- It's important to welcome new people into the circle, so what do you have to do to make room for others to join?

- What can you do to help others feel welcome?

- How many friends can you name, who are in your friendship circle?

Prayer

God, everyone needs friends. Remind us to be willing to step back and make room for more friends to join our circle. Amen.

Company's Coming!

Sweep off the welcome mat,

Add a leaf to the table,

Grab another chair

If you are able.

Today we celebrate,

One and all,

Company's coming,

And the house will be humming!

The bell rings,

And the door swings open.

Every family brings

Something scrumptious to share,

Joy and love are in the air!

The time has come

To gather and eat.

The feast is ready,

And all are on their feet.

Forming a circle, hand-in-hand,

We bow our heads and offer a prayer,

How blessed we are with plenty to share.

Sparks

• What do you enjoy most when family and friends gather?

• "Hospitality" is a fancy word for welcoming others into our homes and hearts. Who welcomes you into their hearts?

• With whom do you enjoy sharing "hospitality" — welcoming into your home?

• What is something you can do to make someone feel welcome when he or she comes to visit you?

Prayer

Gracious God, you welcome us into your household with open arms! May we be eager to welcome people into our family and circle of friends. Amen.

Room at the Table

It was a sunny Saturday afternoon,

Greg and friends were playing football,

While little brother of one of the guys,

Sat on the curb watching the ball

Sail through the sky.

"Let's prepare dinner for everyone!" said dad,

And mother agreed.

So, the two went to work preparing the feast.

The table was set, and all were ready to eat,

But a problem was soon discovered:

Instead of there being room for ten,

There were plates and chairs for only eight!

Quickly, extra chairs were added at each end.

Now there was room for all the friends!

When later asked about the meal,

The little brother didn't mention to his mother,

Steak or potatoes, or the fancy tableware,

What impressed him most,

Was that everyone had a chair.

Sparks

• How does it make you feel when others make room for you to sit at the table with them?

• What do you enjoy about eating with your family and friends?

• What do you know about Jesus's table and his special meal?

• Who is welcome at Jesus's table?

Prayer

Thank you, Jesus, for making room for all of us at your table. Remind us that everyone is welcome at your table. Amen.

Lesson 13

Humility

Putting Others First

Do nothing from selfish ambition or conceit, but in humility regard others as better than yourselves. Let each of you look not to your own interests, but to the interests of others.

Philippians 2:3–4

Putting Others First

Putting others first is thoughtful and kind,

It's a way of letting friends know

Their welfare is on our minds.

It's also a way of showing respect,

Opening the door for others to enter,

Waiting when a friend is lagging behind,

Helping the new kid by inviting him

To join us in line.

A fancy word for putting others first,

Can be read in a Bible verse:

"Do nothing from selfish ambition or conceit,

but in humility regard others

as better than yourselves."

To regard someone as "better than yourself,"

Simply means a willingness to step aside,

And help someone else move up from behind.

Humility is putting needs of others before our own,

Like, letting guests fill their plates first,

When they're in our home.

Humility is also listening without interrupting,

When others speak.

Admitting to ourselves, as well as them,

What they have to say matters to us

And not just to them.

Sparks

• What can you do to put others first on the playground?

• When someone lets you go first, how does it make you feel?

• When someone is speaking, what do you need to remember to do, and what do you need to remember not to do?

Prayer

God, you created and love all the people of the world. Remind us that everyone is important to you. Help us to practice "humility" by considering what's best for other's first—before we consider what's best for ourselves. Amen.

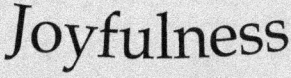

Joyfulness

Shouts of Joy!

… Then our mouth was filled with laughter, and our tongue with shouts of joy… The Lord has done great things for us, and we rejoiced.

Psalm 126:1–3

Quiet Joy

My soul is satisfied as with a rich feast, and my mouth praises you with joyful lips…for you have been my help, and in the shadow of your wings I sing for joy. My soul clings to you; your right hand upholds me.

Psalm 63:4–8

Shouts of Joy!

When gratitude fills our hearts,

Like helium balloons

Our spirits soar.

There are no words glorious enough,

To express the depth of joy within.

Suddenly, shouts of joy bubble up,

We scarce can hold them back.

Bursting forth, they fill the room,

And our hearts are blessed

With a jubilant tune!

Taking flight on the wings of a song,

Shouts of joy erupt as a rapturous refrain!

Shouts of joy will not be constrained!

Soaring to the heavens in a nanosecond,

Shouts of joy beckon the attention

Of the celestial choir,

Chiming in, the chorus continues,

Shouts of joy now abound.

The entire heavens resound with God's glory!

Sparks

- What's the most excited you've ever been?

- What do you do when you're filled with joy?

- What would be a wonderful song to sing when you're so happy that words alone are not enough?

Prayer

Dear God, sometimes we are so grateful we don't know what to do! When we sing and dance with joy, please accept it as our praise, for we know that you delight in our attempts to glorify you. Amen.

Quiet Joy

Joy doesn't spring from toys or things,

Joy flows from a wellspring of love,

Love we're given from God above.

God comforts us when we're sad,

Consoles us when we're mad,

Counsels us when we're confused,

And celebrates with us when we're glad!

Sometimes when scary things happen--

Which happen they will--

We experience a joy that floats on a cloud

This joy is soft and never loud,

This joy offers peace in times of chaos,

Reminding us that God is near,

Assuring us we need not fear.

God knows our pain and hears our complaint.

Yet the joy we feel is very real,

It makes no sense based on evidence,

It's the joy that resonates deep within,

Convinced that God is by our side.

Sparks

• How would you describe "quiet joy" to a friend?

• How does it feel to be sad and then someone is able to make you laugh?

• What words can describe what it feels like to be at peace inside yourself?

Prayer

God, we are so grateful to know that whatever happens, you will always be with us. This is why we can smile even when crying, and laugh even when life is falling apart. Our smiles and laughter are evidence of a quiet joy deep within. Thank you, God, for planting joy deep in our hearts. Amen.

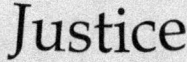

Justice

Fair Play

Happy are those who observe justice, who do righteousness at all times.

Psalm 106:3

Justice for One Is Justice for All

God has told you, O mortal, what is good; and what does the Lord require of you but to do justice, and to love kindness, and to walk humbly with your God?

Micah 6:8

Fair Play

Play isn't just fun and games,

Play is a way we learn,

Whether playing a board game,

Or kicking a ball on a field,

Character and integrity are what we build.

Fair on the field or at the table,

There's no excuse for being hateful,

Controlling our tempers and holding our tongues

Are ways we assure the game is fun.

Anytime we play with another,

Taking turns is something we learn.

Respecting the ones with whom we play

Means being honest in every way.

Friends first and then opponents,

Even though we're on opposite sides,

Our respect for our friends still abides.

Learning to play fair is what it's about,

Learning to be fair is important,

Without a doubt.

Sparks

- What is a game you enjoy playing with friends?
- What does it mean to play fair?
- What does it mean to respect your friends?
- When you're upset, what can you do to control your temper?
- What can happen if we lose our temper?

Prayer

Teach us, Lord, to play fair on the field, at the table, in our homes, and at school. Remind us that our friendships are worth far more than winning a game. Help us control our tempers and hold our tongues when we are upset. Thank you for your Spirit that guides us. Amen.

Justice for One Is Justice for All

Justice is getting what we deserve,

Getting paid

For a job well done,

Getting an award

For a game we've won.

Justice is being fair,

One scoop of ice cream for you,

And one scoop for me, too.

But sometimes things don't go as planned,

Someone gets more than his or her share,

Others shout, "That's not fair!"

This is the time to take a stand.

It takes courage to speak out,

This is no time to pout.

Calmly stand tall

And state your concern,

Give everyone a chance

To have a turn,

Justice for one is justice for all.

Sparks

- What does justice mean?

- When we protect the justice of one person, how does that help everyone else?

- When something doesn't appear to be fair, what can you do?

- Who decides what is fair?

Prayer

God, you want us to treat other people the way we want to be treated. You want us to make good choices and do what is right. Playing by the rules and being fair are what you would have us do. Help us when we're tempted to break a rule to get our way. Remind us that justice for one is justice for all. Amen.

Kindness

Kindness Is Never a Waste

As God's chosen ones, holy and beloved, clothe
yourselves with compassion, kindness, humility,
meekness and patience.

Colossians 3:12

Kindness Is Never a Waste

True kindness treats others in ways

That build them up,

Rather than tear them down.

Cheers them on when they're tempted to quit,

Points out strengths

They'd never admit.

Kindness is defending them

When accused of a wrong

They didn't do.

Inviting them to play,

When others turn away.

Kindness is taking turns,

And letting them go first.

Expecting the best,

When they feel the worst.

Forgiving them,

When they make a mistake.

It's sharing the last donut,

Or piece of cake.

Remember this:

A true act of kindness is never a waste.

Sparks

- What are other acts of kindness that come to mind?
- What is something kind a friend has done for you?
- What makes it hard to be kind sometimes?
- How does it make you feel to do something kind for someone?

Prayer

Thank you, God, for friends who greet us with a smile and are always happy to see us. Thank you for filling their hearts with kindness. Please, fill our hearts with kindness, too. Amen.

Listening

A Riddle: What Do We Pay Every Day?

Let anyone with ears to hear listen!
Mark 4:23–25

Pay Attention

And the king will answer them, "Truly I tell you, just as you did it to one of the least of these who are members of my family, you did it to me."
Matthew 25:40

A Riddle: What Do We Pay Every Day?

What is something we're asked to pay,

Many times, throughout the day?

Rather than pay with nickels and dimes,

We pay with our eyes, ears, and mind.

Here's the last and final clue:

As we watch, wait, and listen,

We're paying it to you.

Sparks

• When you focus on what someone is doing and saying, what are you paying?

• How would you complete the following sentence: "Pay _____. I'm talking to you."

Have you figured out what we're asked to pay,
Not just once but every day?
If not, turn the page…

Pay Attention!

Pay attention to those you love,

Pay attention with smiles and hugs,

Pay attention with a listening ear,

Pay attention to what you hear.

Before I forget, I really must mention,

A sign of respect is paying attention.

So, put down your tablet,

Silence your phone,

Close the laptop

Without a moan.

It's easy to pay attention to our friends,

But there are many hurting hearts,

Attention can mend.

Pay attention to the shy and lonely,

Pay attention to the one who hides behind the tree,

Pay attention to the classmate who never gets chosen.

Pay attention to the one who pretends to be dozing.

Pay attention to the one whose clothes are rumpled,

Pay attention to the one who eats alone,

Remember: We all have attention that we can share,

It's simply a way to show we care.

So, pay attention every day,

Especially to those

Who need it the most.

Sparks

- What are ways you can pay attention to someone?

- How can you tell if someone needs attention?

- How do you know someone is listening when you speak?

Prayer

Loving God, you give us all the attention we need. Remind us that one of the best ways to show respect is to pay attention. Remind us to pay attention to those who are often ignored. Amen

Lesson 18

Loving God

Stack of Bibles

Your word is a lamp to my feet and a light to my path.

Psalm 119:105

Holy Food for a Holy Day

Observe the sabbath day and keep it holy, as the Lord your God commanded you.

Deuteronomy 5:12

Stack of Bibles

Nestled in bed with cozy covers pulled over her head,

Julia was just about to say her prayers,

When in shuffled her big brother, Greg.

Hunched over and straining to stand,

A stack of Bibles he held in his hands.

Counting by twos, the tower numbered ten,

It stretched from his knees all the way to his chin!

Holding them steady with the edge of his face,

Greg explained how he came to be standing in this place.

Room by room he had scoured the shelves,

Raffled through cabinets and searched under beds.

He made it his mission to find one and all.

I, as his mother, was duly impressed!

Puffed up and beaming with pride,

I felt extremely blessed.

I eyed all the Bibles now gathered in sight,

Then patting my back I smiled with delight.

I was soaring to cloud nine like a kite in flight,

When suddenly Greg's words

Yanked me back down to earth:

"You'd think with so many Bibles in this place,

We wouldn't be letting them go to waste."

No doubt about it, my son was right.

A stack of Bibles, no matter their wealth,

Are worth very little when left on the shelf.

Sparks

- Do you know where to find a Bible in your house?
- What is a story or verse from the Bible that you like?
- What have you learned about Jesus from the Bible?

Prayer

The Bible is your word, Lord, and we are grateful to have it. Thank you for letting us get to know you through the stories and instruction it offers, but sometimes it's hard to read. We need you to help us understand what you want us to learn and remember. Amen.

Holy Food for a Holy Day

Someday, when you're all grown up,

I wonder what you'll remember,

When you hear the word "church."

I hope a smile creeps across your face,

I hope your eyes begin to twinkle,

And your heart is filled with grace.

I hope you'll get a warm-fuzzy feeling,

Beginning with your nose,

And traveling to the tip of your toes.

I hope when you hear the word "church,"

A sweet taste fills your mouth,

And holy food is what you're thinking about.

Perfectly round with a hole in the middle,

Puffy and sweet, ready to eat.

Donuts are the ultimate Sunday morning treat!

Donuts are holy food for a holy day.

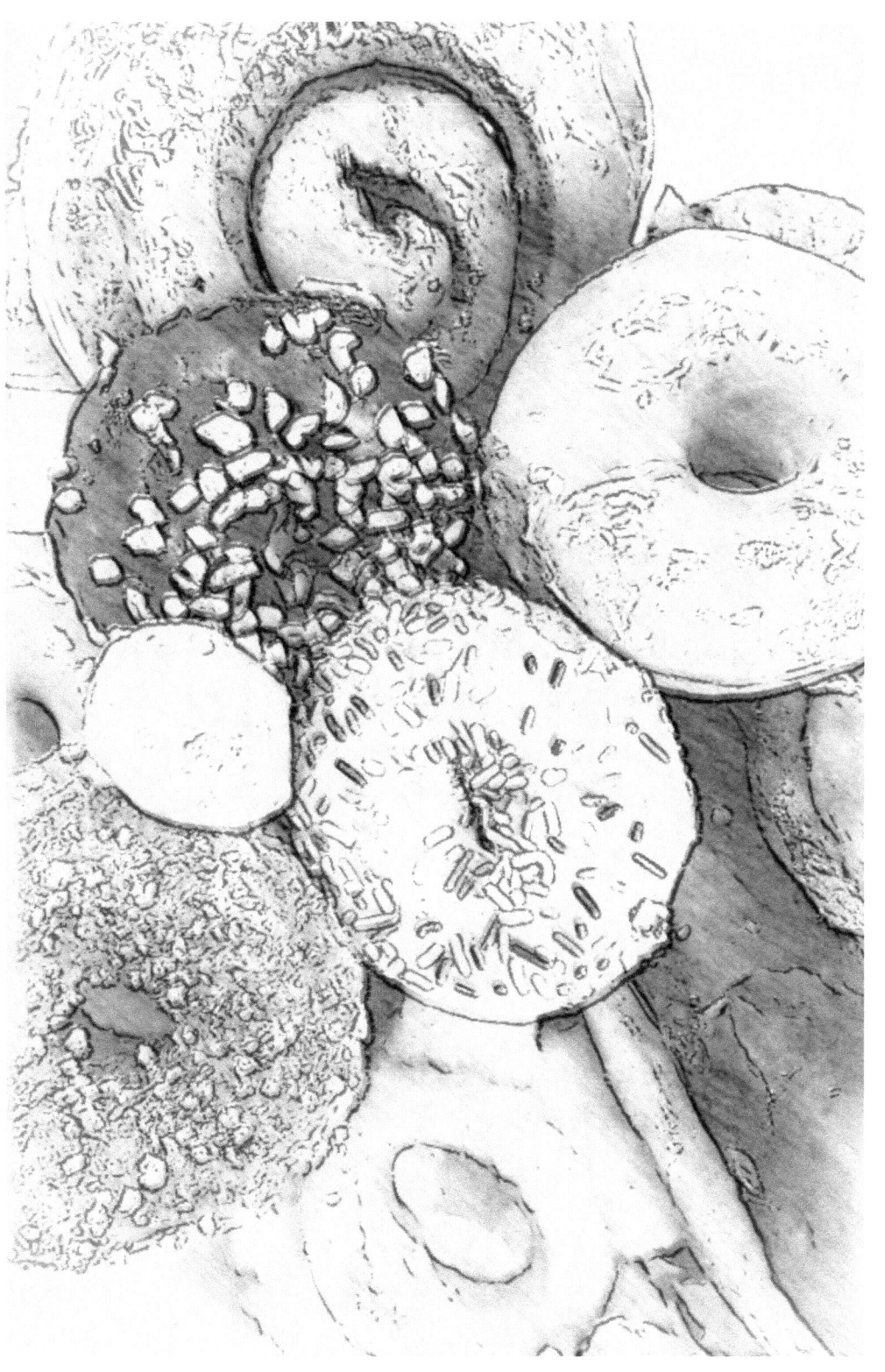

May each bite — or the sight — of a donut today,

Remind you of the tender compassion,

And sweet kindness, of our Maker,

Whose abundant love knows no bounds,

Like a donut, it goes round and round.

Holy food for a holy day.

Sparks

• The word "holy" means something is reserved for God's use.

• Sunday is a "holy" day — reserved for God. What do we do to spend time with God on Sundays?

• We are "holy" because we are God's children. How do others know we belong to God?

• How does God use donuts to remind us that we are loved?

Prayer

Thank you, God, for making Sunday a holy day — reserved for you. Thank you for making us holy — your very own children. Thank you for making donuts holy — a reminder of your never-ending love. Amen.

Loving Others

Love in Action

And let us consider how to provoke one another to love and good deeds, not neglecting to meet together, as is the habit of some, but encouraging one another, and all the more as you see the Day approaching.

Hebrews 10:24–25

Friends We Haven't Met Yet

Let love be genuine; hate what is evil, hold fast to what is good; love one another with mutual affection; outdo one another in showing honor…Contribute to the needs of the saints; extend hospitality to strangers.

Romans 12:9–13

Love in Action

Love is more than a feeling
That makes our hearts flutter,
It's like a rudder on a ship or boat,
Steering us in the right direction,
Teaching us ways to show affection.

Love is wanting the best
For our sisters and brothers,
Wanting what's best
For our dads and our mothers,
Love is wanting the best for our friends,
Not just something they want on a whim.

Love is more than a word,
It motivates us to serve,
Eager to show how much we care,
We serve with warmth whatever we share.

Love is treating others with respect,
Not just wanting what we expect.

Love is listening for their hearts' desires.

Most of all, love is wanting God's best for them,

Even enemies, family, and friends.

Sparks

• What is God's desire for bullies or people we consider our enemies?

• When have you wanted something that wasn't best for you?

• What do you think God's desire is for you?

Prayer

God of Love, we know you want the best for us. Give us hearts for loving each other as you love us—completely and without hesitation. Amen.

Friends We Haven't Met Yet

"Stranger" can be a scary word,

But have you heard?

Strangers are simply

Friends we haven't met yet.

Anyone we don't know

Can become a friend,

It's up to us to welcome them in.

Turning a stranger into a friend

Begins with a smile,

And a happy "hello,"

Invite them to play,

And see how it goes!

Who knows, the stranger we meet,

May become our new best friend.

No matter how young or old,

We can never have too many friends,

Or so I've been told.

Friends are welcome in our lives,

Not only are they fun,

They're often wise.

Friends advise us when we're stumped,

Friends can cheer us when we're grumps.

Before you refuse to welcome a stranger,

Remember this:

You, too, are a stranger to those you don't know,

And…

The best way to make a friend is to be a friend.

Sparks

• What are wise rules to follow when meeting a stranger?

• What can you do to help someone new at your school feel welcomed?

• When you are new to a group, what can you do to make friends?

Prayer

Thank you, God, for friends. Remind us that strangers are friends we haven't met yet. Help us welcome new friends with a smile and a happy hello. Amen.

Loving Yourself

Only One You and Only One Me

Whoever is slow to anger has great understanding. But one who has a hasty temper exalts folly.

Proverbs 14:29

The Best Version of You

In everything do to others as you would have them do to you; for this is the law and prophets.

Matthew 7:12

Only One You and Only One Me

We share many things in common:

Two eyes and a nose,

A couple of ears,

Ten wiggly toes.

But did you know we're each unique?

There's only one you,

And only one me.

There are no two people exactly alike,

Even twins have differences,

Though they be slight.

Because we are different,

You and me,

Our opinions may clash from time to time,

But that's no excuse to let tempers climb,

We each can speak what's on our mind.

Stand up for what you believe,

But always leave space for other's views,

Listen and learn all you can,

Humility and respect go hand in hand.

Sparks

- What is something you like about being you?
- What is something you like about me?
- Humility and respect both value listening. Why is listening to others so important?

Prayer

Thank you, God, for making each of us one of a kind. When we disagree, remind us to listen to each other so we can better understand one another, and our friendship can grow. Amen.

The Best Version of You

There's much to learn when you're a child,

Like brushing teeth, buttoning clothes,

Combing hair, and blowing your nose.

It's a lot to remember,

From head to toe,

But the more you do it,

The smoother it goes.

There are other things you need to learn,

Like being kind,

Taking turns,

Telling the truth,

And always looking on the bright side.

Tougher stuff you learn with time,

Like making decisions

In the blink of an eye,

And acting with wisdom on the fly.

Becoming the best version of you

Means carefully choosing

What you say and do.

Choose to be thoughtful,

Honest and helpful,

Choose to say thank you,

To show you are grateful.

The more you behave a certain way,

Is who you become day by day.

Sparks

• What's something hard you're learning to do?

• What words do you want your friends to use to describe you?

Prayer

Dear God, I want to please you by being the best version of myself. Teach me how to be kind, caring, and friendly in all I say and do. Help me treat others the way I want to be treated. Amen.

Lesson 21

Loyalty

True Blue Friends

O give thanks to God, for God is good; God's steadfast love endures forever!

Psalm 118:1

True Blue Friends

To have a friend is to be a friend,
A loyal friend means keeping promises,
Being honest, protecting and caring
Of one another.

A loyal friend calms us when we're scared,
And if someone dares us to do wrong,
A loyal friend encourages us to be strong.

A loyal friend seeks to understand,
Even when things don't go as planned.

Being a loyal friend sometimes requires
Standing in when our friend is out—
Let's say…
Out with the flu!
Suddenly, no one knows what to do,
No one, that is, except you!

You've been helping your friend
Prepare for a play,

Reciting the lines every day.

Only you know exactly what to say.

This is your chance to really shine!

More important than what it'll do for you,

Is what it will mean to your friend with the flu.

Many say…

"Loyal friends are true blue!"

Sparks

• Who is a loyal friend to you?

• How have you helped a friend when they've needed you?

• I wonder what it means to say "Loyal friends are true blue."

Prayer

God of love, teach us what it means to be a loyal friend. Most of all, teach us how to be loyal to you. Amen.

Patience

Waiting Isn't a Game

God, the one and only — I'll wait as long as he says.
Everything I need comes from him, so why not?
Psalm 62:1 (The Message)

While You Wait

And see, I am sending upon you what my Father promised; so stay here in the city until you have been clothed with power from on high…
Luke 24:49–52

Waiting Isn't a Game

I've heard it said that waiting is a game,

But I say this can't possibly be true.

Who ever heard anyone exclaim,

"Let the waiting begin--we want nothing to do!"

Games are designed with laughter in mind,

Waiting is a countdown--

One boring minute at a time.

If waiting is a game, count me out!

"WAIT!" my mother shouts,

Did she just tell me to wait? I gasp.

Waiting is something I refuse to choose!

"Too bad, so sad," my mother says,

"Waiting is something we all must do," adding,

"Learning to wait is expected of you."

Babies wait to be rocked and fed,

Children wait to be tucked into bed,

Grownups wait for the workday to end,

Grandparents wait 'til they see us again!

Waiting with patience is a God-given virtue.

Whether you know it or not,

God is preparing to work through you

In amazing ways,

But first it's important to learn how to wait.

Sparks

- What is something you're waiting to do?
- How does it make you feel to wait?
- What is something that helps you wait patiently?

Blessing

As you wait, may God bless you with an active imagination so you can envision ways to make the world a better place to live.

As you wait, may God bless you with a brilliant mind to solve a problem that is bothering you or someone you love.

As you wait, may God bless you with helping hands to knit a hat or collect food for someone who is cold and hungry.

As you wait, may God bless you with a grateful heart by reminding you of all the many gifts God has given you. Amen.

While You Wait

Waiting is never easy,

Whether you're four or eighty-two,

Waiting is very hard to do.

Here are a few activities

To help you pass the time.

Waiting doesn't have to be

A boring waste of time.

When waiting for a traffic light

To turn from red to green,

How many pleasures can you name

That make your dear heart sing?

When waiting at the grocery store,

Count the items in your basket,

Ask for a nickel for each can or package,

Then donate the money to the poor.

There's much to do when waiting outside,

It's a perfect time to notice what nature provides.

Listen for birds and rustling leaves,

Sit in the shade of your favorite tree,

Enjoy the caress of a gentle breeze,

Give thanks to God for all of these.

Waiting isn't a waste of time,

Depending on how you use your mind.

Maybe your brain could use a break,

Waiting offers a time to meditate.

Rest your eyes, let your thoughts escape.

Draw a deep breath, and patiently wait.

Sparks

• What do you enjoy doing while you wait?

• What is something you can do as you wait that pleases God?

Prayer

Dear God, thank you for giving us imaginations to help us dream and do things that make you happy while we wait. Amen.

Lesson 23

Perseverance

Just Keep Trying

I can do all things through him who strengthens me.
Philippians 4:13

Cheer Us On!

Therefore, since we are surrounded by so great a cloud of witnesses, let us also lay aside every weight and the sin that clings so closely, and let us run with perseverance the race that is set before us, looking to Jesus the pioneer and perfecter of our faith…

Hebrews 12:1–2a

Just Keep Trying

There's a first time

For everything we do:

Learning to talk,

Leaning to walk,

Learning to skip,

And learning to hop.

The first few tries,

We seldom get right.

So, just keep trying,

With all your might.

If you get discouraged,

As we're all apt to do,

Just picture Jesus

Cheering for you!

God's world is broken,

There's much we can do.

It may mean having to learn something new.

But be assured,

Learning is something you can do.

Just keep trying with all your might,

With practice you're bound to get it right!

Sparks

• What is one of the hardest things you've ever learned to do?

• How did it make you feel the first time you did it?

• What is something you're learning to do now that takes practice?

• How does it make you feel to know Jesus is cheering for you?

Prayer

We have lots to learn, God, and sometimes we want to give up. Help us to just keep trying again and again. When we're about to quit, may we see Jesus cheering for us. Amen.

Cheer Us On!

When the task we need to do is hard,

When what we need to learn a struggle,

There's no need to quit or throw a fit,

Like a puppy in distress,

This is the time to yelp for help!

Family and friends will surely pitch in,

Offering words to help us win,

Speaking words we most need to hear,

Words that are music to our ears,

Words reminding us

We're not alone.

There's certainly no need to complain and moan,

These are words to cheer us on:

"Stick to it!"

"You can do it!"

"Hang in there!"

"We really care!"

"Push ahead!"

"Carry on!"

"Do what you have to do!"

"We're here for you!"

Sparks

• What are words that cheer you on?

• When you're discouraged, what helps lift your spirit?

• What can you say to a friend who wants to give up and quit?

Prayer

Sometimes life is hard, Lord. Sometimes we want to quit trying. Please remind us to ask for help, and when there are others who need a boost, remind us to cheer for them to keep on trying until the end. Amen.

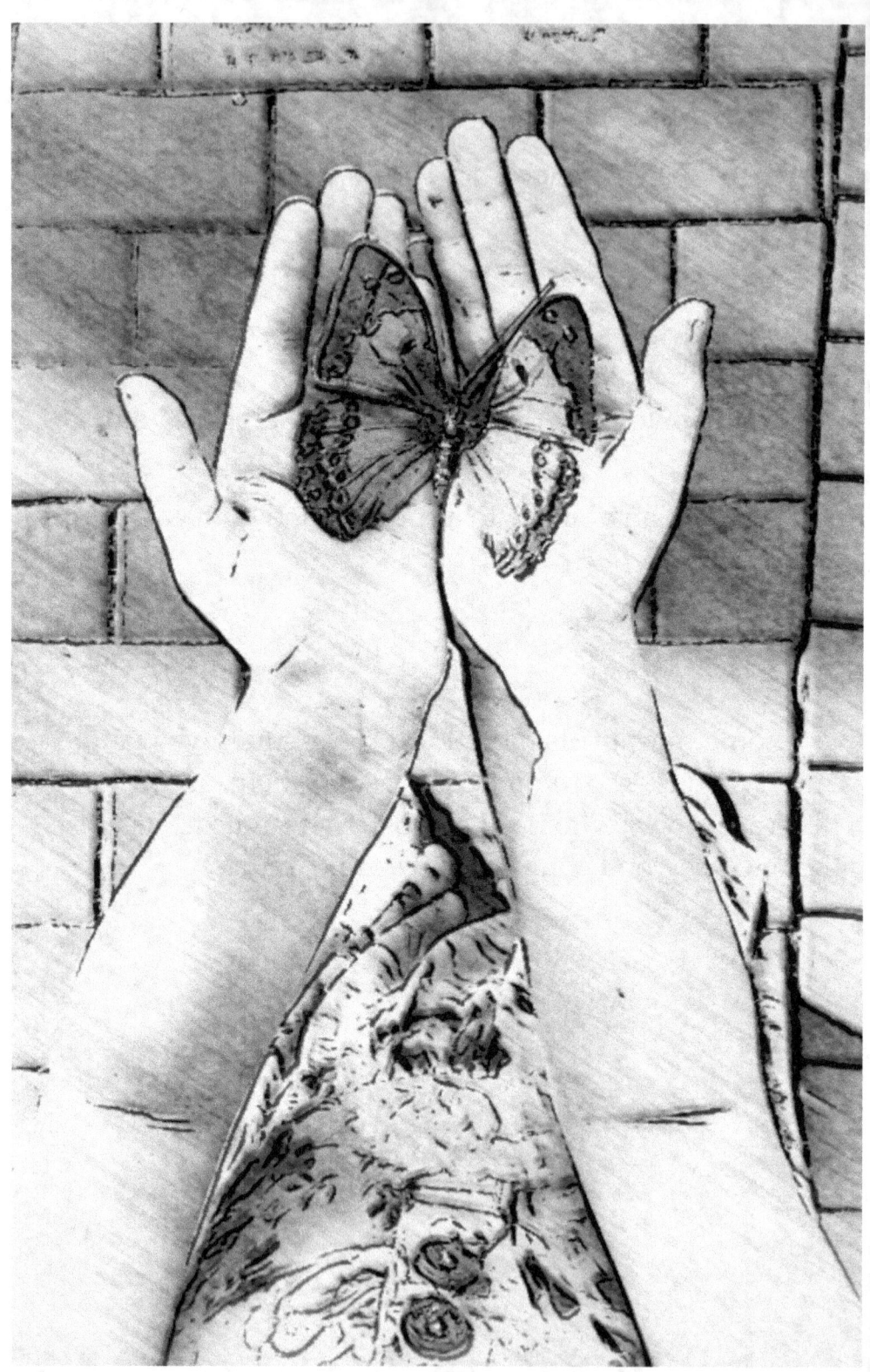

Respect for Creation

Caring for God's Creatures

And God said, "Let the earth bring forth living creatures of every kind...And it was so. God made the wild animals of the earth of every kind, and the cattle of every kind, and everything that creeps upon the ground of every kind. And God saw that it was good."

Genesis 1:24–25

Caring for the Earth

Then God said, "Let us make humankind in our image, according to our likeness; and let them have dominion over the fish of the sea, and over the birds of the air, and over the cattle, and over all the wild animals of the earth, and over every creeping thing that creeps upon the earth"...God saw everything that he had made and indeed, it was very good.

Genesis 1:26–31

Caring for God's Creatures

What's the tiniest living thing you've ever seen?

Was it as small as a speck of dust?

Did it crawl or could it fly?

Did you see it in your house,

Or outside under the big blue sky?

It's amazing to think,

As tiny as it is,

God gave it breath so it can live.

Roly-poly bugs,

Geckos and lizards,

Birds of the air,

And all that have feathers.

People and pets,

Butterflies and bugs,

God made them all,

With a great deal of love.

It's up to us,

As stewards of the earth,

To care for the creatures

Sent from above.

Sparks

• What is the smallest creature you've ever held in your hand?

• I wonder why God made spiders and roly-poly bugs.

• What does it mean to be "stewards of the earth?"

Prayer

Creator God, you are amazing! You have created everything that lives, and you call it good. Thank you for creating us and loving us. Remind us, every day, to appreciate each other and all the animals and creatures you've created and love. Amen.

Caring for the Earth

God created the earth,

And declared it good,

Assigning its care to humanity,

To see that it continues to be beautiful,

Productive, and safe.

Adam and Eve were the first stewards,

Charged with tending the earth.

Every generation since then—

Including all of us—

Is expected to do our part,

Starting where we are,

And doing what we can.

Picking up litter on the school yard,

Conserving water when we wash our hands,

Planting a tree where birds can live,

Trees that will grow and eventually give shade.

Planting bushes and shrubs,

Giving butterflies what they need to eat,

Erecting retaining walls

Along the banks of the creek,

Filling the bird bath with fresh water,

Filling the feeder with an assortment of seeds.

Caring for the earth is what we're called to do.

Caring for the earth is up to me and you.

Sparks

• What is something you do to take care of the earth?

• What would you like to do to make the world a better place?

Prayer

God of Earth, Sea, and Sky, you have created the entire universe and given us the opportunity to join you in caring for it. Thank you for trusting us to care for it. Teach us what we can do to do our part. Amen.

Self Control

Why the Tree?

And the LORD God planted a garden in Eden, in the east; and there he put the man whom he had formed. Out of the ground the LORD God made to grow every tree that is pleasant to the sight and good for food, the tree of life also in the midst of the garden, and the tree of the knowledge of good and evil… And the LORD God commanded the man, "You may freely eat of every tree of the garden; but of the tree of the knowledge of good and evil you shall not eat, for in the day that you eat of it you shall die."

Genesis 2:8–9

Choices

Love is patient; love is kind; love is not envious or boastful or arrogant or rude. It does not insist on its own way; it is not irritable or resentful; it does not rejoice in wrongdoing, but rejoices in the truth. It bears all things, believes all things, hopes all things, endures all things.

I Corinthians 13: 4–7

Why the Tree?

In the beginning God created the world,

And filled it with all living things,

Plants, animals, fish, and people, too.

God created a beautiful garden in the land of Eden.

Here the first humans had everything

They would ever need

To live happily ever after,

But something went wrong…terribly wrong.

In the garden were trees, trees, and more trees.

There were fruit trees, shade trees,

And some trees that bore nuts.

Adam and Eve could eat from any of the trees--

Except one.

This one tree was in the center of the garden,

And of it they were never to eat.

They were even forbidden to touch it!

I wonder, why did God even create this tree?

Why did God plant it in the center of the garden

For all to see?

I wonder, did it ever occur to Adam or Eve

That all they had to do was chop down the tree?

If the tree were chopped down,

the temptation would be gone!

Wouldn't life be much easier without this tree?

Sparks

• What do you think of this story?

• What do you do when you are tempted to touch or eat something you've been told you can't have?

Prayer

God, it's not always easy to keep from touching things we're told not to touch. It's not easy to stop our hands from reaching for a piece of chocolate when we know how delicious it tastes. It sure makes life hard to be surrounded by so many temptations. Please teach us how to turn from temptation and go the other way. Amen.

Choices

In the beginning God created people instead of puppets.

God gave people brains and voices instead of strings.

God gave people hearts that beat.

And feelings to care.

God gave people the ability to share.

One of the best gifts God gave people,

Was the gift to make choices.

Not only do we get to choose

What we do and who we know,

We also choose what we wear and where we go.

More important than any of those,

Is something we wear but it's not our clothes.

Can you guess what it is?

I'll give you a hint:

It's something we wear that always shows.

It's our attitude—how we think and how we act!

It's up to us the attitude we choose.

Choose to be kind. Choose to be thoughtful.

Choose to be patient. Choose to be joyful.

Choose to be loving when others are rude,

Choose to be honest, hopeful, and true.

What attitude do you choose to wear?

The choices you make, eventually make you!

Sparks

• When you choose a cheerful attitude, what kind of person does this make you?

• When someone gives you a gift, what do you choose to say? What kind of a person does this make you?

• What attitude does God want you to wear when someone is mean to you? What kind of person does this make you?

Prayer

Dear Heavenly Father, thank you for teaching us what attitudes to wear. Help us remember that it's more important to choose the right attitude, than what sweater or shoes to wear. Amen.

Trust in God

Other Side of the Door

If I take the wings of the morning and settle at the farthest limits of the sea, even there your hand shall lead me, and your right hand shall hold me fast.

Psalm 139:7–10

Handmade by God

For it was you who formed my inward parts; you knit me together in my mother's womb.

Psalm 139:13

God Answers When We Call

See that none of you repays evil for evil, but always seek to do good to one another and to all. Rejoice always, pray without ceasing, give thanks in all circumstances; for this is the will of God in Christ Jesus for you.

1 Thessalonians 5:15–18

God's Fingerprints

I praise you, for I am fearfully and wonderfully made.

Psalm 139:14–16

The Other Side of the Door

Have you ever seen the movie Monsters, Inc.?

If so, what did you think?

If you haven't seen the movie, I'll tell you more:

In the movie there are lots and lots of doors.

Every door leads to someone's room

Somewhere in the world.

One door might lead to a little girl's room in Texas,

Another door might be to a little boy's room

On a desert island or even on the moon!

No matter where the doors may lead,

The other side of every door is Monsters, Inc.

When I imagine the other side of my door,

I don't imagine monsters,

But something much, much, more…

I imagine God on the other side of the door!

Think about it:

Since God is everywhere,

The other side of the door can be anywhere.

No matter where I live or where I roam,

God's door is always open to welcome me home.

Sparks

- Where in the world do you like to imagine living?

- What do you imagine it's like on the other side of the door — where God is?

- How does it make you feel to know that God is always close to you and God's door is always open to welcome you?

Prayer

Dear God, thank you for always being with us no matter where in the world we are. Remind us that even though we can't see you, you are everywhere and your door is always open to welcome us home. Amen.

Handmade by God

Based on Psalm 139:1-13

O Lord, you have searched me and know me.

You know when I sit down and when I stand tall.

You know what I am thinking before I speak at all!

You know everything about me.

In fact, you know me better than I know myself!

You made my heart, my lungs, my brain,

And all my inward parts.

Like a puzzle, you fit each piece together

And put it in its place,

Then with great care, you wrapped me in skin

And gave me a face.

What a gift it is to be handmade by you!

Maybe that's why you never let me out of your sight --

That's right.

There's no playing hide-and-seek with you.

You know where I am at all times.

Even if I hide in the darkest closet under the stairs,

You find me there.

Dark isn't dark to you.

Night is as bright as day!

If I take the elevator to the top floor

Of the tallest building, you are there.

If I go down, down, down, into a canyon

Or cave under the earth, you are there.

If I fly to the moon or the other side of the world,

you will hold my hand and lead the way.

You surround me and watch over me

Every minute of every day.

What a gift it is to know you care.

What a gift it is to know you're always there.

Sparks

• How does it make you feel to know that God knows everything about you?

• Imagine being in your favorite place with God. Where are you and what are you doing?

Echo Prayer

Dear God, (repeat)
you know where I am (repeat)
and what I'm doing (repeat)
at all times. (repeat)
I hope you're proud of me. (repeat) Amen.

God Answers When We Call

Praying to God is easier than talking on the phone,

No device is needed--there's nothing to hold.

No number to memorize--nothing to know.

Just start talking—that's all we have to do.

"Hello God, it's me. How are you?"

There's certainly no need for caller ID.

God knows our voices and calls us by name.

Whether we speak or simply breathe deep,

We can even call God when we're half asleep.

There's no need to plan what to say,

God answers our calls anyway.

How do we know when God answers our calls?

Sometimes we ask and hear nothing at all.

The answer might be seen rather than heard,

Delivered by a stranger we meet,

Or a bird's fallen feather that lands on the street.

Sometimes the answer comes as a thought,

Other times it comes as a lesson we're taught.

God speaks through the Bible

And also through prayers,

God speaks through events and others who share.

Whether we hear him at once

Or it takes days and days,

This we know: God works in mysterious ways.

Sparks

• What kinds of things do you talk to God about?

• Can you think of a time when God has answered your call? If so, what did God say or do?

• When do you pray?

• Remember: We can call God (pray) anytime, anywhere, for any reason. God is always ready to answer our call.

Prayer

Hello God, thank you for always being ready to listen to us when we want to talk to you. Teach us how to listen for what you want to say to us. Please give us the faith to trust that you always hear us when we pray. Amen.

God's Fingerprints

What in the world makes you different from me?

We both have 10 fingers, and 10 wiggly toes.

We each have a tongue and even a nose!

It could be our hair or maybe our clothes.

Surely, it's something much deeper than those!

Do you smile when you're happy?

Cry when you're sad?

Jump up and down when you're angry or mad?

It's more than our feelings that make us unique.

In so many ways it's a mystery we seek.

Listen carefully as I tell you the secret—

the secret of what makes you different from me:

With a gentle touch and creative flair,

God's fingerprints prove we're made with care.

Sure, we're different yet so much the same.

God even knows us each by name.

We're all works of art--you and me!

Shaped and fashioned by God's loving heart.

Sparks

• What is something about you that God made special?

• What is something about me that God made special?

Echo Prayer

Dear God, (repeat)
thank you for making everyone unique (repeat)
and special in some way. (repeat)
Help me to recognize your fingerprints (repeat)
on myself and others. (repeat)
Thank you for touching our hearts with love. (repeat)
Amen. (repeat)

Greg's Memory of a Life Lesson: Hospitality

The first day of each session of church camp followed a familiar pattern. Children and youth from throughout the presbytery and beyond would arrive, choose cabins, and head to the swimming pool. This would be followed by meeting cabinmates and general milling around until the old church bell rang, indicating that it was time to gather at the dining hall for supper. A playful prayer would be sung, lasagna would be eaten, and just before the children and youth were dismissed to gather with their new "family groups," my mom would perform a feat that perplexed all of us counselors.

She would stand up and walk from table to table and, strictly from memory, name each individual camper, counselor, and staff member – this could be anywhere between 30 and 60 people. In a matter of a few hours and based solely on introductions and brief conversations, she would know each individual by name –- as well as which little West Texas town most of the campers had come from.

When asked how she remembered everyone's names so quickly, her response was simple yet profound: "Because children are important, and children's names are important to them." She placed value on each child's identity and made it a priority to ensure they felt seen and known. This act of hospitality will always stay with me.

Sometimes we become too focused on the "how" of things and overlook the more significant "why." In the case of my mom's ability to remember names, it was not about strategies or techniques she used. Instead, it was about understanding the importance of making each child feel valued and recognized.

This is just one example of the lessons that I have learned as witness to my mom's ability to embody the often overlooked spiritual gift of hospitality. Through her example I have learned that, sometimes, the "how" is insignificant compared to the "why," and that it is in creating an atmosphere of love and acceptance where the "hows" naturally/divinely unfold.

Greg Six

Afterword

Julia's Memory of a Life Lesson: Inclusion

 The countdown to a birthday is very important for many of us, especially when we are children. The anticipation of what gift you'll ask for: Barbie or roller skates; what kind of cake you want: chocolate or strawberry; what will the activity be: bounce house or a craft; and of course, a theme – you must pick the perfect theme to set the tone of the party. A multitude of decisions need to be made, but one decision that never needed to be made in our household was the guest list. It was simple: Invite your entire class. When asked to write about a life lesson Greg and I grew up learning, this was the first to pop into mind.

The lesson of inclusion and making everyone feel wanted at the party was consistently stressed. Now, I don't remember if this rule to invite everyone was ever attached to a biblical scripture, but for me, it has always been tied to what God wants us to do for others: Love them, accept them, and include them in the joy and celebration of his love!

To this day, when planning a party, I try my best to include as many as possible on the guest list, knowing that some may not be able to attend. The point isn't to have a giant party, but to make sure no one feels left out, which reminds me of the "rule of thumb" in our family: Abundance is a good thing! If by a miracle everyone RSVP's "yes", no problem. I just buy a bigger cake and make sure I have enough party hats for everyone!

Julia Six Aldriedge

About the Author

Rev. Dr. Janice Six

 Born and reared in Abilene, Texas, Janice is a third-generation member of First Central Presbyterian Church (FCPC) where her grandparents joined in 1925. It was here that she was baptized and confirmed, married, and ordained as a deacon and elder before being ordained as Minister of Word and Sacrament of the Presbyterian Church (USA) in 2005. Janice is the first female to be installed as a pastor at FCPC.

Prior to entering full-time ministry, Janice taught Family and Consumer Science in public schools, which included courses in child development, and marriage and family living. She joined the staff at FCPC as the Director of Christian Education in 1997 and retired in 2022 after 25 years of service.

Janice is married to Gene Six, and they have two children, Greg and Julia—both baptized and married at FCPC. Greg is married to Trudy, and Julia to Jace. Greg and Trudy's daughter, Greer Louise, is the first of the fifth generation to be a baptized member of FCPC. All live in Abilene and are active in the church family.

Janice has a Master of Divinity degree (M.Div.) from Abilene Christian University's Graduate School of Theology and a Doctor of Ministry degree (D.Min.) from Louisville Presbyterian Theological Seminary.

www.ingramcontent.com/pod-product-compliance
Lightning Source LLC
Chambersburg PA
CBHW060523130626
46553CB00002B/626